WHEN ANXIETY WON'T LET GO

From Panic to Peace

A guidebook from one who has been there.

CAROLINE BEIDLER, MSW

SMART LIVING IN SMALL BITES

TABLE OF CONTENTS

Published in the U.S. by: The Grit and Grace Project
Address: P. O. Box 247
        Estero, FL 33929
Email: info@thegritandgraceproject.org
Web Address: www.gritandgracelife.com
Author: Caroline Beidler, MSW
Editor: Ashley Johnson
Special Projects Manager: Allison McCormick
Photo credits: All photos courtesy of Shutterstock and Unsplash

This book is written by the author to share her life experience with the sole purpose of providing insight, encouragement, and hope. The information provided in this book is for informational purposes only and is not intended to substitute professional counseling or treatment.

The Grit and Grace Project®
#gritandgracelife

ACKNOWLEDGMENTS

This is my most favorite part to write in any book. It's a time to sit and contemplate gratitude. It is also a chance to humbly acknowledge all of the many hands that are involved in the crafting of a book, however big or small, weighty or humorous.

To my husband, who chooses to walk alongside me during every season, from the challenging ones to the peaceful ones.

To the ladies of Grit and Grace Life, especially Darlene, Ashley, Allison, and Tess: You all are amazing. Thank you for your vision for this project, your grace in the revision process, and your heart for women. God works in all of you mightily.

Thank you to my recovery family and my church family who are one and the same these days. Without you, I'd be untethered and disconnected, and this is never a good look on me.

I also want to acknowledge and thank Lindsey, who walked alongside me during a challenging bout of anxiety in 2020. You helped me find myself again.

And finally, to you, sweet reader. Thank you for joining me on this journey. You are so worth every second of the work. As my friends in recovery like to say, "Don't give up before the miracle happens."

DEAR READER

Welcome. However you are showing up today, I want you to know I am so glad you are here. I believe (because I've experienced it) that sometimes we are guided to something because we need to be. This book is here for you in this moment, right now, for a reason. And I am here, too.

As a woman in recovery from all sorts of things, like mental health challenges, addiction, ice cream, and binge-watching "Yellowstone" (because I am also in recovery from cowboys) and who is also an author, social worker, and recovery expert, I know firsthand how debilitating a struggle can be—especially a mental health challenge like anxiety.

For me, it's been an uphill climb to learn how to live with a free mind and to keep it free. I've learned some things along the way that I'd love to share with you, and most importantly, I've learned a few of the secrets to smart living that you will learn as you work your way through this guide. In these pages, you will find an interactive experience, space to share your own thoughts, and more.

You may be short on time (as a mom of littles, so am I!). You may be hesitant to address anxiety in your own life, and you may even question if a book like this is for you. I'd like to encourage you to push through the doubt, trust the process, and believe that you and your well-being are worth it. Because you are so very worth it, dear friend.

With hope for your journey,

Caroline

MY STORY

When I've had an anxiety attack in the past, it felt something like this:

Tunnel vision.

Heart out of rhythm.

Mouth drying out.

Hands and feet going numb.

Mind set on one thing: I am going to die.

We are going to die.

This is never going to end.

I remember my first hot yoga class—someone let out a long sigh. The heat and my current season of life (stress-filled graduate school), led me to run out of the room. At a full sprint to grab my bag, I didn't even make eye contact with the fit, young yogi who was looking very concerned behind the counter asking, "Are you OK?"

Don't stop.

Get. Out. Of. There. Fast.

Next stop: Target. My line of thinking at the time: *What's better for a panic attack than shopping?*

I made it to the parking ramp, opened my door and sat there and breathed.

Breathe.

Breathe.

Do I need to call 911?

I almost called 911.

In my purse, I had the emergency bottle of anti-anxiety medication they can prescribe to someone who says, "I am in addiction recovery; please do not give me anything addictive." Though I recognize I can make pretty much anything addictive. Ten to 15 minutes later, I can breathe.

Breathe.

Breathe.

Again. Slow. Purposeful.

This Can Be Cured, Right?

After this incident in my early 30s and years of struggling with anxiety (and what I didn't know at the time was generalized anxiety disorder), I started seeing a therapist again regularly. I started taking medication. I prayed. I read my Bible. I went to a small group. I was even in recovery for addiction (this is a topic for another day). I did all the things I thought were going to cure me—or at least make the anxiety less debilitating. There were even people (well-meaning people) in my life who said things like:

"You just need to pray more."

"You need to trust God more."

"You are living in fear, not faith."

But what I heard was, "You are the problem." And from this, I inferred that I am the only one who can fix this.

Still Not Working

So, I did all the things and then more. More therapy. More medication. More prayer. And yet, more anxiety as the world felt like it started turning in on itself at the beginning of 2020.

Here's an example: We stepped out of church smiling, ready to make Sunday ours, but as soon as we opened the thick oak doors and our faces touched the air, I knew.

Something was on fire.

I looked over to the mountain ridges and there was an eerie, hazy smoke that rested like watercolor paint in the gray sky.

"Cover your mouths and noses with your shirts," I told my children. "Let's hurry to the van."

They rushed, and I called my husband.

"Have you been outside? Can you smell the smoke?" I asked.

Calling my husband is like a check and balance for me. Is this real? Sometimes I need him to reassure me that it is and I am not losing it.

Over the phone, I hear the back porch door open and the dog bark, and then, "Oh my God," he says after a few seconds. "Fire."

Our small, eastern Tennessee town was surrounded by fire on all sides. One hundred-acre fire here, 500-acre fire there. All county firefighters were at the scene. Since Saturday.

How had we not heard about this? I called some friends, and they were oblivious, too.

Why is no one telling us the world is on fire?

I looked around and noticed the birds were gone.

We spent Sunday indoors with the air filter on, and when we had to let the dog out, we covered our faces.

I thought about the recent fires in Canada and how all over the news there were pictures of the Eastern United States in a yellow-orange bubble of smoke. People wearing masks. People standing still, looking confused. Articles online about how to make a homemade air filter using paper towels, box fans, and duct tape. Googling "wildfire preparedness" and printing off a checklist. Having conversations about what to put in a go-bag if there is an evacuation. Thinking back to elementary school in the 80s when my favorite teacher told me about the Amazon rainforest and about how we had to stop cutting down trees and burning all this energy.

"We have to stop now," she said.

And that was the 1980s.

If you are feeling anxious right now, I'm sorry. And me too.

This is a small glimpse into the reality that so much of the world is facing: natural disaster, man-made disaster, disease, wars, the stuff our kids see online. There is enough of the world to make us all want to jump in bed, pull the covers over our heads, and pretend that we can make it all go away if we keep our eyes shut and tune out the noise. What's worse is that we, as women, are still supposed to carry on as if it's OK to not be OK.

When We Are Supposed to Have it All Together

The pressure for women is real. It doesn't matter if we are just starting college or even high school. It doesn't matter if we've just married a dreamy, lanky young man or if we are waiting for our Prince Charming (whether in Wranglers or a three-piece suit), if we have children or an empty nest. It doesn't even matter if we go to church in the upstairs pews or in the basement spaces where people talk about their struggles with addiction. We are showing up today. Wherever we are showing up from, I think there is an expectation that women are supposed to have it all together.

I will be the first to admit that I don't have it together, but believe me when I say that it's been a slow process of learning to be honest about how I'm feeling inside. And even still today, the darkness can come creeping back in and tempt me to hide my feelings and struggles.

We are supposed to have it all together because, let's face it, women are wearers of many hats. We are mothers, daughters, sisters, friends, neighbors, church committee members, PTO participants, cupcake makers, birthday-present buyers, cleaners, cookers, toy picker-uppers, drivers, confidants, counselors, and nose wipers—just to name a few.

We are also supposed to be caring, but not overly emotional. Empathetic, but boundary experts. Seasoned, but not gaudy. Beautiful, but not show-offs. And, God forbid, we make any other woman feel less than just because we are more.

We are supposed to have it all together, but let's face it—we don't.

Anxiety is something that is just going to happen sometimes because we are living in an anxiety-inducing world. Our primordial selves have the fight-or-flight responses kicking in because we are human. We are created to self-preserve; to endure.

Yet, when things like anxiety creep in (a natural human response or a heightened human response), this can only add to the pressure to be perfect—and the guilt that follows when we aren't. Of the many hats we wear, struggling with anxiety or anxious thoughts cannot be one of them.

But why?

And, most importantly, how can we overcome it?

I believe that when we understand where we are coming from and how we got the dirt under our nails (the dirt being anxiety in this image), we can move into a place where guilt can turn into honesty, and honesty into peace.

After we are able to gain clarity, then true, deep healing can follow. In the next part of this book, I'm going to show you how.

"Anxiety isn't a sin. It's an emotion. It's what you do with the feeling of anxiety that leads you to healthy or unhealthy places."

— Debra Fileta, M.A., LPC

YOUR STORY

Every person's story is nuanced. Yet, we share a common hurt and need. Telling our own story—even if it's just for ourselves to read—is an important step toward hope and healing. This is a space where you can share how anxiety has shown up in your own life. List examples of what you've experienced or perhaps a couple of memorable times that have stuck with you.

PROBLEMS TO FACE

I'm going to put my "recovery expert" hat on for a moment and share some things I've learned about anxiety.

Anxiety can stem from your physical health and hormonal changes, or it can be a part of a response to trauma and stress due to an underlying mental health condition. Whatever your "why," know you aren't alone. Anxiety is a real issue for many women today. It's helpful to explore the underlying issues and then seek solutions. It can also be helpful to listen to another person's experience and reflect on your own story. After reading each of the following examples from my story, note the similarities and differences from your experiences. What thoughts, questions, and/or feelings arise as you read?

Low Self-Esteem and Self-Worth

As I've vulnerably shared in these pages, anxiety has led to me feeling not good enough. I've let anxiety decide how I see myself and how I determine my intrinsic worth.

Has anxiety caused you to think less of yourself?

Strained Relationships

Mental health challenges, like anxiety, can cause stress in our lives, and it's not surprising that this can spill into our relationships. When I called my husband about the wildfires, he was (and is) thankfully healthy enough to know how to respond. He listens and then asks if I'd like advice, support, or just an ear to hear me. It's taken several years for both of us to practice how to communicate and how to show up for one another. Anxiety has caused me to withdraw from relationships and isolate because I've felt ashamed of being anxious and afraid to ask for help and talk to anyone about what I was experiencing.

How has anxiety impacted your relationships?

Physical Health Issues

If you are still reading, I don't have to tell you what anxiety feels like or what it does to the mind and body. You are here because you know and have experienced it. For me, anxiety has led to a whole series of unpleasant symptoms: racing heart rate, insomnia, mental fogginess, and additional symptoms that create a web of increased worry, fear, unease, or apprehension. Experiencing a fight-or-flight response out of nowhere and for no apparent reason on the surface can be more than discouraging; it can be downright debilitating.

What are some ways anxiety has impacted your physical health?

Avoidance and Missed Opportunities

The physical symptoms of anxiety and the emotional ones, like fear have led to my avoiding and missing opportunities to connect with others. For years, the thought of being vulnerable with others or even speaking in social settings sent my systems into overdrive. I was ready to bolt at the thought of having to be in a room of people, even people I knew. When I've struggled with anxiety, I've missed things like social events, friends' birthdays, family gatherings, and more.

Have there been times in your life when you've missed out because of your anxiety and its related symptoms?

Shame

Shame can be very destructive and can keep us from living in gratitude and showing up for others. I've already shared that I've felt less than because of my anxiety and have experienced being covered in shame because of it. I used to tell myself repeatedly that I was "crazy." It was a label I felt like I just couldn't escape. I also felt shame because I never felt like I belonged in circles of what I viewed as healthy or "normal" people. Going to church and participating in women's ministry events or small groups sent my mind racing and my heart palpitating because I never felt like I belonged with people who appeared to have it all together.

What are some ways that you've felt shame about your struggle with anxiety?

After reading through some of the problems and issues I've faced with anxiety and reflecting on your own, I hope you can recognize the truth that you are not alone in your experience. Anxiety is something so many of us deal with, and it can be more than challenging.

For many of us, it creates low self-esteem and self-worth, strained relationships, physical health issues, missed opportunities, shame, and more. What's worse, sometimes our loved ones exacerbate the problem when they don't understand and try to offer platitudes like "have faith" or "just pray more."

But you are not alone! Check out some of these statistics that remind me I am not the only woman on the planet who experiences anxiety:

You Aren't Alone:
- Anxiety disorders rank as the most prevalent mental health condition in the United States, impacting over 40 million adults, which constitutes 19.1% of the population. [1]
- The most frequently occurring anxiety disorder in the U.S. is generalized anxiety disorder (GAD), affecting 6.8 million adults. [2]
- Younger individuals, particularly those between 18 and 24 years old, are more prone to experiencing symptoms of anxiety, with nearly half reporting either depressive disorder or anxiety symptoms. [3]
- Women are more than twice as likely as men to grapple with an anxiety disorder. [4]
- Despite anxiety disorders being highly treatable, more than 60%

of individuals affected do not seek treatment. [5]

Importantly, sweet reader, this is not the end of our stories! Now, I'd like to guide us (I'm working on this, too!) to a place of re-framing the idea of anxiety from a problem to an opportunity. Challenges are something we have to deal with, but opportunities are something to welcome and ultimately learn from. With opportunities, there are steps we can take to heal.

I recognize you might be experiencing feelings that I have not captured. I have given you space below to write about your emotions and reflect on how they are impacting your life today.

"You may not control all the events that happen to you, but you can decide not to be reduced by them."

— Maya Angelou

STEPS TO TAKE

What can we do when anxiety strikes or when we are weighed down by panic?

You may be in the middle of your battle with anxiety, unsure where to turn and feeling like you are drowning in your symptoms. You may be working your way to the other side with a mental health professional, but needing some extra support and yearning to hear your own story reflected back in another's experience.

As *Grit and Grace Life* founder Darlene Brock shares in her *Smart Living in Small Bites* book, *When Suicide Touches Your Life*: "No matter where we find ourselves on this journey, there are things we can do and truths we can discover that will lead us to the road of healing."

Over the next several pages, I'm going to share steps we can take together that will help us move into a new place of healing and freedom from anxiety. I've been there. God has brought healing and wholeness to my mental well-being. Is every day perfect? No. Do I still struggle sometimes? Yes. But today, I have the tools, and I can't wait to share more with you about how I've been able to walk in freedom one step at a time. Connected now by our experience, I'd love to ask you to continue on this journey to free our minds from the destructive fears that can hold us back.

I'm also going to offer up some practical tools and insights. After that, there will space for you to reflect and journal as you address the anxiety in your own life. Woven throughout will be biblical affirmations for recovery, along with tools from the mental health and addiction recovery community.

Consider these warm blankets and cups of lavender tea when you feel like your anxious mind needs a reset or encouragement because, sweet friend, I can say with assurance—it does!

Low Self-Esteem and Self-Worth Became Boldness

Anxiety became such a normal part of my life, for years I didn't realize the grip it had on me. I thought everyone nibbled their nails down to bloody cuticles. I thought everyone had sweaty nights of racing thoughts and sleeplessness. I was sure that everyone looked down on themselves as someone "too broken" and "crazy."

What I didn't know was that because of some of the things I'd experienced in my early years—like my parents' divorce, then sexual trauma, and likely because of a family history of mental health challenges—some pretty heavy things weighed on my young mind. I didn't know how to cope with life and its shrapnel in healthy ways. And, because of this, my self-esteem was in the gutter.

In his second letter to the Corinthians, the Apostle Paul teaches us to "take captive every thought to make it obedient to Christ." [6]

I love this verse, and I remember the first time I heard it. I realized there were actions I could take to promote my well-being and that I didn't have to be held captive by the anxious thoughts swirling—I could release them to God. The more I learned this and practiced it when anxiety came creeping back into my life, the more I gained courage and even boldness. I started to see myself not as someone defined by her anxiety and struggles, but as an imperfectly beloved child of God.

Friend, what if instead of putting ourselves down because of our anxiety or anxious thoughts, we counter the negative self-talk and thought patterns with this alternative: State what's going on, and then share aloud who we are in God's eyes. Let me show you an example of an exercise to try when you are feeling anxious:

First, take a deep breath and say, "Right now, I am feeling anxiety." Recognize it. Notice it. Take another deep breath and say, "I am still a beloved child of God."

Repeat this as many times as necessary. *Freedom in Christ Ministries* offers a helpful resource with more "Who I Am" statements that can be helpful to replace negative thinking and self-talk around anxiety. [7]

After trying this exercise, write down your thoughts. What happened to your anxiety? What happened to your thinking?

Strained Relationships Became Practicing Vulnerability and Openness

When I became a young adult, anxiety caused me to want to retreat, impacting my relationships. If I didn't know when anxiety or a panic attack were going to strike, I hesitated to be around anyone for fear of what they might think or what I might look like. Anxiety led me into a season of crippling self-consciousness. So what led me from strained relationships—or non-existent ones—into a new season of community? Sharing.

In my late 20s, I started going to an outpatient treatment center for my substance-use challenges. Not knowing how to cope with my anxiety and other mental health symptoms, I turned to self-medicating with substances.

At this treatment center, I started group therapy and went to these groups twice a week. Here, I was with other people who struggled too, and we were encouraged to share what was going on in our lives. At first, it was excruciating. It was terrifying to talk in a group of people, let alone share my feelings. Every week I showed up, and every week when it was my turn to talk, I opened up a little more.

After some time, I noticed something incredible: The more I shared and the more vulnerable I became, the more I connected with others. Today, nearly 20 years later, the people I met in those rooms are some of my best friends. Vulnerability led to not only freedom from anxiety but also a beautiful and supportive community.

Now, you may be feeling anxious even thinking about going to treatment for your anxiety, so I'm going to reassure you that there are many pathways to healing, and this might not be for you. What can be practiced by anyone no matter the location is opening up and sharing with another human being, and continuing to do it. Over time, something beautiful is going to bloom.

Try this: Call a trusted friend, mentor, pastor, or family member, and share what's going on with you. Talk about your anxiety. Set a reminder on your phone or calendar to call this person weekly (or even daily!). After a couple of months, note how you are feeling or what happened.

Physical Health Issues Became Prioritizing Self-Care

Anxiety doesn't just impact my mental well-being; it can affect my physical health as well. For me, this can look like loss of sleep and a loss of appetite—stomach churns and burns and other digestive issues that shall not be named here. You may be able to relate to the evergreen need for Pepto-Bismol, or you may have your own physical health symptoms that pop up. However anxiety shows up in your body, whether it's stomach-related or maybe makes your shoulders and neck muscles feel like a rubber band about to snap, research shows that anxiety doesn't just impact the mind.

What I've learned through this is that instead of letting this make me feel bad about or for myself, I can reframe it this way: It's time for some self-care.

When anxiety causes physical symptoms, we can counter them with physical actions. Gentle movement like walking or stretching, or even quick movement like CrossFit or running, can help calm the nervous system and ease physical anxiety symptoms. Other calming activities like prayer, meditation, or even strolling the mall (yes, that can still be a thing)—anything that helps you get out of your own head—can help.

Take some time to list ways that anxiety shows up for you in your body. Then, share some ways you lovingly care for yourself. If you are having a difficult time writing ways that you can be loving toward yourself, imagine you are giving advice to a dear friend. What would you tell her? How would you encourage her to take care of herself? Let's be friends to ourselves. Your list is now an action plan to follow when your anxiety symptoms are stifling.

Avoidance Became New Opportunities

As I mentioned before, anxiety in the past led me to isolate myself from relationships. I was ashamed and felt so alone in my experience. Especially when I became a Christian, I thought I was supposed to have it all together.

Because of the way I isolated myself, I missed out on so many opportunities to build relationships. I practically ran from anything that felt like a healthy connection: friends in high school, sports, college roommates, opportunities to travel oversees for missions, even jobs. There were many opportunities where I allowed my anxiety and fear to take hold.

Today, I am so grateful. Because of the community I'm part of and the way I've been able to connect with others through my vulnerability, incredible opportunities have presented themselves. And because I am committed to my healing, I am present for them, too.

Writing this book, for example, happened because I stepped out in courage several years ago to share words with Grit and Grace Life. I worked through the fear and anxiety of wondering, Am I good enough? to know that when I leap into the unknown, I can trust God has a plan.

What are some ways you have avoided good things like connection or other missed opportunities because of your anxiety?

To be present for new opportunities, I'd like you to consider that you can learn how to lean on others and trust. We can do this by reflecting on our social support or support circles. Who do we have in our corner that can help us move from a place of anxiety to a freeing place of choice?

Take some time to reflect on your support network. Using the diagram on the following page, write the names of those in your inner circle in the circle #1. This will probably be only one or two people. These are your go-to folks, your ride-or-dies. In the circle #2, share the names of the people you connect with regularly, but who aren't super close. Finally, in the circle #3, write the names of the people you'd like to build a stronger connection with. Note that some of these people are likely to share your experience of anxiety. (Remember, you are not alone.) Now, beside the circles, write five ways you can intentionally connect with your supports regularly. You might just find that new opportunities will present themselves, and you will be present for them.

#1

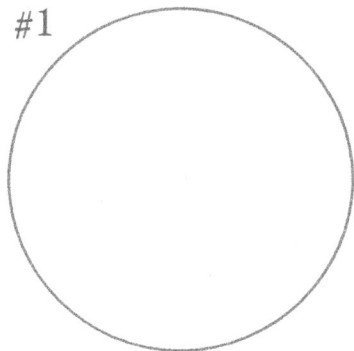

#2

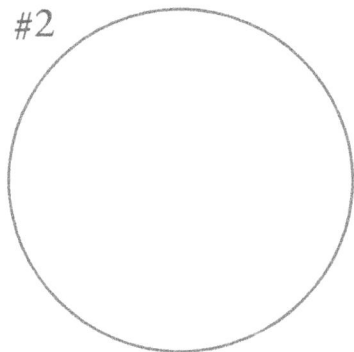

#3

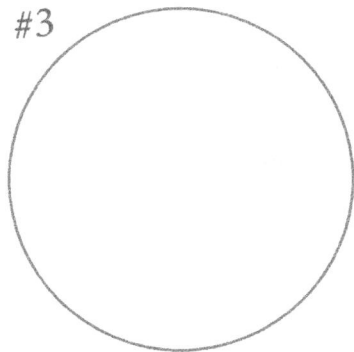

Shame Became Embracing Gratitude

Gratitude is one of the most powerful gifts I have received through my own journey with anxiety. Today, instead of seeing anxiety as something that is causing my life to be overwhelming or debilitating, I can view it with new eyes. Having anxiety has led me to so many gifts, like learning how to connect with others and discovering new passions and dreams. My journey with anxiety recovery is one where I am brought daily—sometimes moment by moment—in utter awe of the way God and connecting with other human beings in community have healed me.

I'm going to encourage you now to do something that might feel strange at first: Write a gratitude list for your anxiety. What are some things that you are thankful for? Note that this might be challenging, but reframing anxiety as an opportunity can give us a new mindset! We don't need to stay stuck in shame. For me, anxiety has led to developing healthy practices like daily exercise and prayer, which is all-around good for a balanced life. What are some ways anxiety has presented opportunities in your life?

Our days are short. We have the agency to choose whether we're going to attach to the shame of mental health challenges, like anxiety, or view them in the light of opportunity and healing. We can embrace a new identity that leads to freedom.

We may not be fully delivered from anxiety, but we may learn important ways to show up more presently. How are you going to show up for others today? Think back on your circles of support. How can you be a part of someone else's circle?

"You are worth every second of the work."

– Caroline Beidler, MSW

FINDING HOPE

My struggle with anxiety started as a young child before I had the words for it, long before I tried hot yoga or the time my town was surrounded by wildfire. My struggle with anxiety was born out of an unstable childhood, worry-prone genetics, and post-traumatic stress. When I became a mother, anxiety multiplied as if it were the triplet to my twins. I remember leaning over their double bassinet, praying to God their little chests would keep rising and falling. I watched their little chests rise and fall every night for hours and days. Sleep was like a distant relative you never see.

What I've learned over time is that there is a name for what I am feeling when my mind starts swirling and my heart starts beating. When anxiety strikes. And more importantly, I've learned there are actions I can take to alleviate the unruly and oftentimes debilitating symptoms. Therapy, medication, community, recovery, and God's work in my life have all combined for my good and continue to work so I don't have to live in fear today. And even when I do get anxious, I don't have to let it control how I think about my worth, my life, or my ability to show up for the ones I love.

In 1 Peter 5:7 in the Bible, Peter shares this: "Cast all your anxiety on him because he cares for you."

When Peter penned these encouraging words, the people of that time were overwhelmed by war, plagues, persecution, famine, and a region hostile to new Jesus followers (not unlike our world today). When they were written, Peter's words were a welcome balm.

We can take comfort in knowing that as we struggle with things like anxiety or even other troubles of the world, we are not alone. Generations have lived with anxiety.

Chuck Swindoll from *Insight for Life Ministries* shares this insight from the book of 1 Peter:

"It isn't enough for us to simply get up every morning and trudge through each day; neither is it advisable to paste a smile on our faces and ignore troubles. Instead, the lesson of 1 Peter is to push through the troubles, recognizing their temporary presence in our lives while walking in holiness and hope as people of faith." [8]

We can take comfort in knowing we have a loving Father we can cast our anxiety upon. I like to imagine my anxiety is in giant grocery bags, and instead of me solo-hauling the groceries into the house alone, God can take a bag or two. We don't have to carry anxiety's heavy load. We can live with hope and a free mind.

Want more biblical truth about anxiety? On the next page are a few of my favorite passages of Scripture that point to ways we can find encouragement when we feel anxious.

"For the Spirit God gave us does not make us timid, but gives us power, love and self-discipline." (2 Timothy 1:7)

"I have told you these things, so that in me you may have peace. In this world you will have trouble. But take heart! I have overcome the world." (John 16:33)

"Peace I leave with you; my peace I give you. I do not give to you as the world gives. Do not let your hearts be troubled and do not be afraid." (John 14: 27)

"Cast all your anxiety on him because he cares for you." (1 Peter 5:7)

"'For I know the plans I have for you,' declares the Lord, 'plans to prosper you and not to harm you, plans to give you hope and a future.'" (Jeremiah 29:11)

"Fear not, for I am with you; Be not dismayed, for I am your God. I will strengthen you, Yes, I will help you, I will uphold you with My righteous right hand."

— Isaiah 41:10

FINDING YOUR HOPE

On the lines below, take inventory of any areas where your faith feels weak and record any opportunities you see for growth. Consider writing a prayer to God for his help, perspective, and strength.

WHEN MEMORIES RETURN

As I shared earlier, I think sometimes we women feel like we need to have it all figured out—show no weakness and carry on no matter what. And when we get support or see a therapist or start a medication for our mental health, we are expected to be instantly cured.

The reality is that mental well-being and healing from anxiety is a journey, not a forever "peaceful easy feeling." Sometimes anxiety comes back. Memories of the anxiety come back. Tough times return, sometimes even more challenging than before.

It is during these times we need to remember that we are human. No human is immune from trial or challenge, anxious thoughts and/or panic. There is a lot to be anxious about in our world today. Anxious thoughts will return, and that's OK. The difference is that when we work on our mental health and follow the suggestions in this book, we can find recovery moment by moment.

We can also reach out for additional support. I strongly encourage you to explore other options for mental health support, including counseling. We are never alone in our experience.

"*Therefore do not worry about tomorrow, for tomorrow will worry about its own things. Sufficient for the day is its own trouble.*"

– Matthew 6:34

BEFORE YOU GO

Before we part ways for now, I want to encourage you that you have access to this resource at any time. You can look back on what you've written at different points in your life, too, and see how you've changed or progressed along your journey of healing. You can share your thoughts with a friend. You can even work with a small group through some of the questions or exercises.

The exciting part about healing is that it is up to us. There are too many things in this world that we can't control and many that cause sweat to form on our palms or our hearts to start racing—and yet, there is good news. We can choose healing. We can show up for ourselves. We can have compassion on our experience and open our hearts to a God who loves us no matter what. No matter our anxieties, fears, or concerns: We are held.

Praying with you for your peace and continued healing,

Caroline

"Our anxiety does not empty tomorrow of its sorrows, but only empties today of its strength."

— C.H. Sturgeon

THE HOPE
WE'VE FOUND

This guidebook is a reminder that every woman's life is a journey. Every one of us will face good times and hard times. We all have stories that we love to tell and stories that still hurt to remember. While our human experiences may have similarities, there is no one who truly understands what you have been through and who you are better than Jesus. And he wants to invite you further into another journey—a faith journey—with him.

If you are searching and encountering him for the first time, we trust you will meet the Savior who gave all through the most difficult times because he had his love set on you. If you already know him and are building your relationship with him, we believe he will sustain you. If you have felt disheartened by the despair life can bring, we want you to know that God is not disappointed in your doubts or struggles—but is only more drawn to you in his tender mercy.

No matter where you are in your faith, God wants to meet you there. To be your hope and help. And we want you to know that he truly will.

Heather Jonsson, one of the Grit and Grace Life team writers, has unpacked each step of our faith journey: beginning faith, battered faith, and building faith. They are all a part of the faith journey the writers at Grit and Grace Life are on.

We hope that her written invitations will help you join us on this path that leads to a sense of purpose in this life and holds promise for the one to come.

Also, if you enjoy Heather's writing, we encourage you to find more of her personal work at www.heatherjjonsson.com.

Beginning Faith

I wish you were sitting with me today, here in my living room. Here where the gentle spring winds play with my blue curtains, and the warm sun is melting away the frost of winter. There is a shift in the air.

You and I would take a walk, shedding our coats to allow the sun to kiss our skin. And we would sit outside on the patio, charmed by the green shoots pushing their way through the cold earth, which just last week was blanketed in snow. And I would look in your eyes and tell you, this awakening to life we feel, when what was dead begins to awaken, this is what has happened to my soul as I have come to know Jesus.

Have you ever had a friend who, just by spending an afternoon with them, makes you a better person—happy, full, content? So it is with Jesus. He loves you with an unstoppable, unchanging, perfect love, and his love changes you. This is the beauty of following Jesus. Like the daffodils which, against all odds, burst bright and yellow against a dreary backdrop of spring, this is the perfect work of Jesus' love for you.

Let me offer you a personal example. As a young mother with two small children, I was often angry when my husband had to work late. He isn't a workaholic, but sometimes he couldn't help but have a late evening completing his assigned tasks. When he finally arrived home

I would give him the silent treatment, making sure he understood my anger by my cold shoulder. But I began to realize this was helping no one, and especially not myself as my anger grew like a weed, choking out the joy.

So I decided to use those extra hours talking with Jesus. I would share my frustration and ask for strength in my parenting. I looked for happy moments playing with my small children, and prayed for a patient, loving heart when my husband returned. Slowly, I changed. I became less of an angry wife when my husband walked in the door, and more joyful, happy, patient, and kind in my communication. This is the beauty of following Jesus. It changes us.

Like me, do you find yourself in need of the one who loves like no other? The one whose love changes you for the better? Now understand, following Jesus is not the easy life, ridding you of all difficulties; no matter our journey, the pain of life never fails to sting. However, following Jesus is a deeply fulfilling and rich life in the middle of both the beautiful and the broken.

God's Word tells us that we are needy, and he is limitless. We are broken, and he is the healer. We are deficient, and he is perfect. When we come to fully realize our insufficiency, we can truly see he is what we need.

If I'm honest, I'm still deeply needy and broken and deficient, and there is not a day that passes where I do not reach out asking Jesus to help me. But after years of following Jesus I am less broken and less deficient; now I am more whole, stronger, and at peace with myself and others. Jesus' love has cocooned me and changed me from who I was into who he created me to be; it is a process not a potion.

Dear one, is there something holding you back from following Jesus? Please journal your thoughts below.

After that, grab your Bible and look up John 10:10. No worries if you don't have a Bible; just do a quick google search to find it. Consider the life Jesus is freely offering you.

A checklist does not define those who follow Jesus, nor does obedience to a list of rules. Instead, following Jesus cultivates within your heart a blossoming garden, one full of flourishing in a fruitful relationship. A garden tucked away in your soul which even the most fierce of storms cannot destroy.

Here are some comforting realities about what it means to follow Jesus, straight from the Bible:

- "Every person who has walked this earth needs Jesus; he loves us exactly where we are and died for us when we didn't even know he cared. But God showed his great love for us by sending Christ to die for us while we were still sinners" (Romans 5:8, NLT).

- "For he has rescued us from the kingdom of darkness and transferred us into the Kingdom of his dear Son, who purchased our freedom and forgave our sins" (Colossians 1:13-14, NLT).

- "I pray that God, the source of hope, will fill you completely with joy and peace because you trust in him. Then you will overflow with confident hope through the power of the Holy Spirit" (Romans 15:13, NLT).

If you have never said, "Jesus, I want to follow you," then let me invite you to pray these words with me. "Jesus, you alone are the way, the truth, and the life. I believe you died for my sins so I can live. I trust you and I will follow you all the days of my life."

Welcome to new life, dear one! As followers of Jesus, we want to soak up as much sunlight as possible so we can flourish. There are so many ways you can do this, but let me lay out a few steps for you:

- Spend time reading or listening to God's Word. Set a time of the day, and let this habit become a rhythm in your daily life. The timing of this will ebb and flow with different seasons of life, so be mindful that this is a rhythm, not a rule.

- There are many wonderful Bible studies you can purchase, or you can read a few chapters of the Bible every day. I recommend you begin with the book of John, then move to Ephesians. John will teach you so much about Jesus, and Ephesians will teach you so much about Jesus in you. This is a beautiful combination.

What is one step you can take to begin your journey of faith?

BATTERED FAITH

One summer afternoon cloaked in sunshine, my friend and I walked under a brilliant sky that betrayed her dark emotions. In deep grief she turned to me and asked me, "Will I ever trust God again?" You see, together we had prayed and believed God for a pertinent need, only to have her life crumble around her. I scoured my heart for a wise response and came up empty.

Looking back, I wish someone would have told me that trust is much more challenging than one originally anticipates. I wish someone would have said, "Heather, trust will take more courage than you ever imagine." And most importantly, I wish someone would have reassured me that even shaky trust is still trust, like a child learning to walk.

In this season of life, the Psalms became dear to me. The psalmists who spoke in gut-wrenching honesty about their feelings towards God resonated with me. The Psalms they wrote that expressed these emotions are called laments. A lament is defined as a "passionate expression of grief or sorrow." We see them throughout scripture, as they were a way for God's people to bring their complaints before his throne.

There is no formula to a lament, no right or wrong answers. But a general outline looks like this:

- Expression of complaints, grievances, and pain
- Request for God to act
- Statement of surrender and trust because of who God is

Why don't you use the outline above and take some time to write a lament? (If you would like some examples, you can find laments in Psalm 3, 7, 13, 30, 88, 79, 137.)

Lamenting is one way to walk towards healing. Another way, especially when our faith feels feeble, is to swim back upstream and find the ocean where our faith began. We see this evident in Naomi's story found in the book of Ruth, which begins as one big detour of disappointment. Why don't you take time now to read the beginning of Naomi's story in Ruth 1:1-22.

In reading this story, we see that due to a famine, Naomi, her husband, and their two sons, left Bethlehem and moved to the country of Moab. But Naomi's husband died, leaving her alone with her sons. Then, after her two sons married, her sons also died. In lament, Naomi returned to Bethlehem with her foreign daughter-in-law, telling the people of her town, "Do not call me Naomi; call me Mara (meaning bitter), for the Almighty has dealt very bitterly with me. I went away full, and the Lord has brought me back empty."

Yet Naomi did an interesting thing. She trusted Boaz, her family's kinsman redeemer, and placed her future in his hands. The roles of a kinsman redeemer are laid out in the Levitical Law (Leviticus 25). In summary, a kinsman redeemer is a family relative who helps a weaker relative in need, or who willingly pays off the debts of a relative— essentially buying back what was lost due to the debt. From the time Naomi returned to Bethlehem, she knew that Boaz was their close relative and a "worthy man," and Naomi trusted Boaz would uphold the law.

Initially, Naomi sent her daughter-in-law, Ruth, to glean in his fields. Then, after seeing how Boaz protected and provided for Ruth in the fields, Naomi sent Ruth to lay at Boaz's feet while he slept. At the time, this was seen as a request for him to be their redeemer.

But Boaz didn't stop at fulfilling the requirements of the law, he exceeded them. Boaz bought Naomi's family land, fulfilling the law, but then he also married Ruth and had a child with her so Naomi's family line would continue. As Naomi cradled her new grandson, her friends called out a tune far different from Naomi's words that she said upon her return. They said, "Blessed be the Lord, who has not left you this day without a redeemer. He shall be to you a restorer of life and nourisher of your old age."

Naomi, despite her bitterness and despondency, knew her redeemer, and placed her trust in his capable hands. And Boaz was faithful. If this story feels familiar, it should, because Jesus, our Redeemer, repeated this story in our spiritual lives. He is the one who paid our debt of sin by his death on the cross and now calls us his beautiful bride, the ones whom he deeply loves (Isaiah 54:4-8; Revelation 19:7-9).

Like Naomi demonstrated, focusing on the character of God doesn't remove us from this painful world, but it gives us safe harbor through it. So when your life hits a detour filled with disappointment, swim back upstream to the ocean of God's strong character, and saturate yourself in the truth of who God is. He is truly worthy of our trust!

Here are four steps you can take right now:

- Let's see how God defines his character. Look up the verses listed below and note what you learn about God.
  - -Psalm 46
  - -Psalm 96
  - -Ephesians 1:3-10
  - -1 John 4:7-21
- Repeat these to yourself often!
- Declare your surrender at the end of your honest lament.
- Surround yourself with people who will speak truth and hope into your life, like Ruth and Naomi did for each other.

What did you learn about God's character after reviewing the listed verses? Consider writing a prayer of lament in the space provided below.

BUILDING FAITH

Sister, I picture you holding this little book and coming to this last page, a page designed to build and encourage your faith. But what does one say to someone who, by the power of God, has already lived as a mighty warrior? You, who have taken the sword of the Spirit and wielded it with power and precision. What does one say to those already walking in truth and life?

I start by saying what I say to my children after every single one of their sporting events: I love watching you play! In the same way, I imagine Jesus smiling upon you with pure joy and thinking, "I love watching you." I don't think he analyzes your every mistake, nor revisits your slip-ups and failures. Rather, he is over the moon about you!

Just as a buttercup tilts its face toward the sun, we thrive under the loving warmth of Jesus. Revelations 2 is a clear picture of his priority for the saints who endure. Here, the word of the Lord came to the church in Ephesus, "I know your works, your toil and your patient endurance ... I know you are enduring patiently and bearing up for my name's sake, and you have patiently suffered for me without quitting."

But according to Revelation 2:4, "But I have this complaint against you. You don't love me or each other as you did at first!" Where had the church in Ephesus missed the mark?

During my younger years, I ran a few half marathons. Usually I got bamboozled into it by a few friends, and then I was committed. The honest truth is that I did not love running. But I spent the hours necessary for training because it was a free and healthy workout, one where I could buckle my kids into a stroller.

See the correlation? I was like the church in Ephesus, I had everything but love. So unfortunately, my running hasn't outlasted my kids aging out of the jogging stroller. But what if I loved running? I know a few crazy ladies who do! They keep running. And running. And running.

Let me offer you a gentle nudge, something I'm asking myself even as I write these words... In a spiritual sense, where is your first love? Have you, like the church in Ephesus, toiled and patiently endured, but lost this love? Have you noticed any changes in priorities during the years of your maturing faith?

Take a few moments and talk with God about how you loved him, and what, if anything, has changed?

Think back to your younger relationship with Jesus. Maybe it was in college, or as a high school teen, or young adult. How might you maintain the "love you had at first?"

When we love someone, whether it's the love of a friend or the love of a spouse, spending time with that person becomes a priority. So it is with Jesus. To continue deepening our relationship with Jesus, we must continue to spend time with him. When I look back on my life, my closest friends are the ones I talked to most often.

Here are some suggestions to get you started:

- Find a local church where you can be involved. Spend time serving in the church and connecting with the other members.
- If your church does not offer a women's Bible study, connect with one in your local area. Bible Study Fellowship, Precepts, and Community Bible Studies are all wonderful options.
- Develop rhythms of prayer. These rhythms will change throughout our different seasons of life. For example, when my children were little, I used their naptime to write and pray in my journal; now that my children are all in school, I spend my time walking the dog or cleaning the dishes talking with God. Once you have begun the habit of talking with Jesus throughout your day, you will never go back.

Thankfully, in Jesus, nothing is wasted. Nothing is lost. Not even the years of toil and patient endurance.

But let me leave you with this charge: God is love, and whoever abides in love abides in God, and God abides in him. So beloved, let us love one another, for love is from God, and, first and foremost, let us love the Lord our God with all our heart and with all our soul and with all our mind.

What one or two things will you commit to doing to help build your faith?

ABOUT THE AUTHOR

Caroline Beidler, MSW is an author, recovery advocate, and founder of the storytelling platform, Circle of Chairs. She is the author of *You Are Not Your Trauma: Uproot Unhealthy Patterns, Heal the Family Tree*. She is passionate about leading women into greater healing, transformation, and recovery.

With almost 20 years of leadership experience within social work and ministry, she is a consultant with JBS International, a team writer for *Grit and Grace Life,* and a blogger at the global recovery platform *In the Rooms*.

Caroline lives in eastern Tennessee with her husband and twins. She enjoys hiking in the mountains and building up her community's local recovery ministry.

Connect with Caroline on Substack here:

Instagram: https://www.instagram.com/carolinebeidler_official/

Facebook: https://www.facebook.com/carolinebeidlermsw/

Website: https://www.carolinebeidler.com/

RESOURCES

Use this QR code to access a free printable companion journal, additional books related to the topic, and more.

Below are additional books in the Smart Living series.

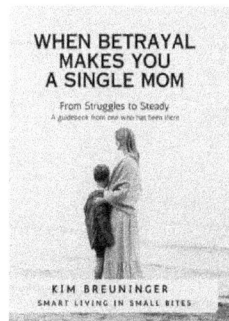

WHEN ANXIETY WON'T LET GO
From Panic to Peace
A guidebook from one who has been there
CAROLINE BEIDLER, MSW
SMART LIVING IN SMALL BITES

WHEN SUICIDE TOUCHES YOUR LIFE
From Hurt to Healing
A guidebook from one who has been there
DARLENE BROCK
SMART LIVING IN SMALL BITES

WHEN YOUR PAST ABUSE STILL HURTS
From Broken to Restored
A guidebook from one who has been there
ALLISON MCCORMICK
SMART LIVING IN SMALL BITES

WHEN MARRIAGE IS HARD
From Conflict to Connection
A guidebook from one who has been there
JULIE BENDER
SMART LIVING IN SMALL BITES

WHEN DATING AGAIN FEELS SCARY
From Fearful to Courageous
A guidebook from one who has been there
MARLYS JOHNSON LAWRY
SMART LIVING IN SMALL BITES

WHEN BETRAYAL MAKES YOU A SINGLE MOM
From Struggles to Steady
A guidebook from one who has been there
KIM BREUNINGER
SMART LIVING IN SMALL BITES

Coming Soon

Other Books

At *Grit and Grace Life*, we strive to bring you great articles every day. Over the years, we've had the honor of sharing practical tips and helpful wisdom with our readers. We couldn't do this without our team of talented writers. Like you, these women are learning to navigate the ups and downs of life with grit and grace.

What you may not know is that many of our writers have dug a bit deeper and written books that can help you (or someone you love) on your journey. Are you ready to change your life?

Use this QR code to access a list of books written by *Grit and Grace Life* writers.

Don't worry about anything; instead, pray about everything. Tell God what you need, and thank him for all he has done. Then you will experience God's peace, which exceeds anything we can understand. His peace will guard your hearts and minds as you live in Christ Jesus.

— Philippians 4:6 - 7

ABOUT GRIT AND GRACE LIFE

Grit and Grace Life is a place for strong women and those who want to be. As a community of women, we have come together to share the life lessons we have learned and the wisdom we have gained. Whether it's through books, videos, social media, podcasts, or on our website, our goal in everything we do is to help women navigate this challenging and wonderful life.

We tackle all things women face, whether big or small, knowing that as we do, we will find strength. We are a collective from every age and every stage of life, here to pass on our stories and the answers we've found through the joys and challenges of our lives. Our driving desire is to provide insights, real-life solutions, hope, and encouragement to all who walk alongside us.

Faith is paramount to who we are and what we do. We have been gently guided in our lives by a God who loves us faithfully and completely. It is in him we find hope and healing. We believe you will, too.

Through all we do at Grit and Grace Life, our prayer is that you would embrace grit and grace as the strongholds of your life, just as we have. And, please, remember this: Grit determines that life challenges won't defeat or define us. Grace gives kindness to ourselves and others, even when it's hard.

www.gritandgracelife.com

This Grit and Grace Life podcast can be heard at:
https://thegritandgraceproject.org/podcast

Follow us on social media:
https://www.facebook.com/ThisGritandGraceLife
https://www.instagram.com/thisgritandgracelife/
https://www.youtube.com/watch?v=mS4O3YC2Ejw

www.ingramcontent.com/pod-product-compliance
Lightning Source LLC
Chambersburg PA
CBHW071627040426
42452CB00009B/1523